Lily and the bubblegum balloon

Kirsten Yates

Published by Kirsten Yates, 2024.

LILY AND THE BUBBLEGUM BALLOON

First edition. August 11, 2024.

Copyright © 2024 Kirsten Yates.

ISBN: 979-8227150172

Written by Kirsten Yates.

Table of Contents

To my dearest Lily Grace,

May this story remind you of the boundless magic within your heart and the endless possibilities that await you. Just as Lily's adventures inspire wonder and joy, may you always find magic in every moment and light up the world with your beautiful spirit.

With all my love,

Mom (Kirsten Yates)

Chapter 1: The Pink Balloon

Lily was a curious girl with a vivid imagination. Every day after school, she loved to explore her small town, finding new nooks and crannies that she had not noticed before. She had an adventurous spirit and a particular fondness for bubblegum, especially the pink, sweet kind. Her pockets were always filled with different flavors, and she could blow the biggest bubbles of any kid in her neighborhood.

One bright, sunny afternoon, as Lily was walking home from school, something caught her eye. On a street she had walked down many times before, she noticed a small, quaint candy store she had never seen. The building was old, with ivy crawling up the brick walls, and the windows were foggy with age. Above the door hung a wooden sign that read **"The Enchanted Confectioner."**

Curiosity bubbling up inside her, Lily decided to step inside. The bell above the door tinkled softly as she entered, and a warm, sugary scent enveloped her. The store was dimly lit, with shelves lined with jars of colorful candies, chocolates, and sweets of every kind. It felt like stepping into a different world.

Behind the counter stood an old man with a kindly face and twinkling blue eyes. His hair was white and fluffy, like a cloud, and he wore a deep purple apron with pockets full of candy. When he saw Lily, he smiled warmly.

"Welcome, young lady," the old man said in a voice as soft as caramel. "What can I do for you today?"

Lily looked around in wonder. "I was just looking for some bubblegum," she replied, her eyes settling on a jar filled with shiny pink gum balls.

The old man chuckled. "Ah, bubblegum! A fine choice. But I have something very special that you might like even more." He reached beneath the counter and pulled out a small, gold tin. It was old and slightly tarnished, with a picture of a bubble on the lid that seemed to shimmer in the dim light.

"What's that?" Lily asked, her curiosity piqued.

"This," said the old man, holding the tin out to her, "is no ordinary bubblegum. It is magical. It has the power to take you on the most incredible adventure, but only if you are brave enough to try it."

Lily's eyes widened with excitement. She loved stories about magic and adventure, and the idea of bubblegum that could do something extraordinary was too tempting to resist. "How does it work?" she asked eagerly.

The old man smiled mysteriously. "Simply chew the gum and blow a bubble. But be warned—if you blow the bubble too big, you might find yourself in a place you have never been before. A place far away far from here."

Lily's heart skipped a beat. An adventure? She asked; A magical place far away? It sounded like a dream come true. Without a second thought, she handed over her allowance money and took the tin from the old man.

"Thank you!" she said, already imagining the adventures she might have.

The old man nodded, his eyes twinkling with a secret knowledge. "Remember, my dear, be careful with the bubblegum. And enjoy your journey."

Lily tucked the tin into her pocket and waved goodbye as she left the shop. She hurried down the street, her mind racing with possibilities. What kind of adventure could a piece of bubblegum take her on?

She did not have to wait long to find out. As soon as she reached the park, she sat down on a bench beneath a large oak tree and opened the tin. Inside were five perfectly round, pink gum balls, each one gleaming softly. They looked just like ordinary bubblegum, but Lily knew there was something special about them.

She popped one into her mouth and began to chew. The gum was sweet, with a flavor that reminded her of strawberries and sugar. As she chewed, she felt a strange, tingling sensation on her tongue, almost as if the gum was alive.

Taking a deep breath, Lily pursed her lips and began to blow. The bubble grew quickly, expanding far beyond the size of any bubble she had blown before. It was perfectly round and smooth, and it floated gently in the air in front of her face, shimmering in the sunlight.

But the bubble did not stop growing. It kept expanding, growing larger and larger, until it was almost as big as Lily herself. She gasped in amazement as the bubble lifted off from her lips and began to float upward, taking her with it!

Lily clung to the bubble, her heart pounding with a mix of fear and excitement. She looked down and saw the ground getting farther and farther away. The park, the trees, the people—they all started to shrink as she rose higher and higher into the sky.

"Whoa!" Lily exclaimed, unable to believe what was happening. She was flying! The bubble was carrying her up into the clouds, and she was soaring through the sky like a bird.

As the wind rushed past her, Lily felt a thrill of exhilaration. This was incredible! She had always dreamed of flying, and now it was really happening. The bubble was so big and strong that it seemed to have a mind of its own, guiding her through the air with gentle ease.

Lily looked around at the world below, which was now far beneath her. She could see the entire town spread out like a map, with tiny houses, streets, and parks. She even spotted her own house, looking like a little toy far below.

But as she floated higher and higher, Lily started to wonder: where was the bubble taking her? How high would she go? And most importantly, how would she get back down?

For now, though, she decided to enjoy the ride. She let go of her worries and focused on the incredible adventure that was just beginning. The sky above was a brilliant blue, with fluffy white clouds floating lazily by. The bubble was glowing softly, casting a pink hue over everything around her.

Lily smiled, her excitement growing with each passing moment. This was going to be the adventure of a lifetime.

And so, with the wind in her hair and the world far below, Lily's journey began—an adventure beyond her wildest dreams, all thanks to a magical piece of bubblegum.

Chapter 2: Floating Over the Town

Lily clung tightly to the massive pink bubble, her heart pounding with a mixture of excitement and nervousness. The ground was far below her now, the park where she had started her journey barely visible. She could see her entire town spread out beneath her like a giant patchwork quilt. The houses looked like tiny boxes, the streets like thin lines, and the people like little dots moving about their day, completely unaware of the girl floating high above them.

The wind was gentle, and the bubble floated smoothly through the sky, carrying Lily higher and farther. She could feel the sun warming her face, and the air up here was fresh and cool. Lily leaned forward slightly, peering over the edge of the bubble to get a better look at the world below. She could see her school, the playground, and even the ice cream shop where she and her friends liked to go after class. Everything looked so different from up here—small, peaceful, and serene.

As Lily drifted over her neighborhood, she waved down at the familiar places, wondering if anyone would look up and see her. She spotted her friend Emma playing in her backyard, her golden retriever chasing a ball. Lily called out to her, but her voice was lost in the wind. Emma did not look up, and Lily realized that she was too high for anyone to hear or see her. It was like she was in her own little world, floating above everyone else.

The bubble carried her further, taking her over the town square where the weekly market was in full swing. Colorful stalls lined the streets, with vendors selling fresh fruits, vegetables, flowers, and handmade crafts. The aroma of baked goods wafted up to her, making Lily's stomach rumble. She smiled as she watched the townspeople bustling about, shopping and chatting. Everything seemed so normal down there, but up here, she was having the most extraordinary adventure.

Lily felt a twinge of nervousness as she realized just how high she was. What if the bubble burst? Or what if she floated too far away and could not find her way back? The thought made her grip the bubble tighter, but then she remembered the old man's words: *"This bubblegum is magical. It will take you on an adventure like no other."* The bubble seemed strong and steady, and there was something comforting about the way it moved, almost as if it knew where it was going.

As Lily continued to float, the bubble began to drift toward the outskirts of town. She passed over the river that wound its way through the countryside, the water sparkling like diamonds in the sunlight. She could see the hills beyond the town, green and rolling, dotted with trees and the occasional farmhouse. The bubble carried her higher still, until she was soaring above the treetops, the town slowly shrinking into the distance.

Lily's excitement started to build again. Where would the bubble take her next? What kind of adventure awaited her beyond the familiar sights of her hometown? The possibilities seemed endless, and the thought made her heart race with anticipation. She had always dreamed of going on a grand adventure, and now, it was really happening.

Suddenly, the bubble dipped slightly, and Lily gasped as she felt herself being gently lowered. She looked around, trying to figure out where she was going, but all she could see were trees stretching out in every direction. The bubble seemed to have a destination in mind, but Lily had no idea what it was. All she could do was trust the bubble and enjoy the ride.

As the bubble descended, Lily caught sight of something strange up ahead. Through the trees, she could see a flash of white—something big and fluffy. Her curiosity piqued, she leaned forward, trying to get a better look. The bubble continued to lower, bringing her closer and closer to the mysterious white object. Was it a cloud? But how could a cloud be down here among the trees?

The bubble drifted gently down until it hovered just above the treetops, giving Lily a clear view of what lay below. Her eyes widened in amazement as she realized what she was looking at. It was not just any cloud—it was a castle, made entirely of clouds! The towers were tall and spiraled, the walls soft and billowy, and the whole thing seemed to glow with a soft, ethereal light.

Lily's breath caught in her throat. She had never seen anything like it. The castle looked like something out of a fairy tale, floating just above the ground, hidden away in this magical forest. And the bubble was taking her right to it!

As she floated closer, Lily could see figures moving around the castle grounds. They were small and delicate, with wings that shimmered in the sunlight. Fairies! Lily's heart skipped a beat as she realized that she was about to enter a world she had only read about in stories.

The bubble finally came to a gentle stop just outside the gates of the cloud castle, and Lily carefully climbed down, her feet touching the soft, cool surface of the clouds. The bubble bobbed in the air beside her, as if waiting to see what she would do next.

Lily took a deep breath, feeling a mix of excitement and wonder. This was the start of something amazing—an adventure she would never forget. She looked back at the bubble, which seemed to shimmer with encouragement, and then turned toward the castle, ready to see where this magical journey would take her next.

And so, with the pink balloon floating by her side, Lily took her first step into the Cloud Kingdom, where her adventure was just beginning.

Chapter 3: The Cloud Kingdom

Lily stood in awe before the grand gates of the Cloud Kingdom. The gates themselves were woven from strands of mist, shimmering softly in the light, and they parted silently as she approached. Beyond them, the cloud castle loomed, ethereal and dreamlike, with its towering spires reaching toward the sky. The air was cool and fresh, with a faint scent of something sweet—like freshly baked pastries mingled with the crispness of a morning breeze.

The pink bubble that had carried her here floated gently beside her, as if encouraging her to step inside. With a deep breath and a heart full of wonder, Lily crossed the threshold into the Cloud Kingdom.

As soon as she passed through the gates, Lily noticed that the ground beneath her feet was not solid like the earth back home. Instead, it was soft and springy, like walking on a bed of the fluffiest cotton. Each step she took left a gentle imprint in the clouds, which slowly rose back up as she moved on.

The Cloud People, whom Lily had only glimpsed from above, were now all around her. They were small and delicate, with translucent wings that fluttered like the wings of dragonflies. Their bodies were made of mist and light, and they glowed softly, like lanterns in the twilight. Some had hair that looked like spun sugar, while others had tiny, twinkling stars woven into their locks.

As Lily walked further into the kingdom, the Cloud People began to gather around her, their eyes wide with curiosity. They whispered among themselves in voices that sounded like the rustling of leaves in a gentle breeze.

"Who is she?" one of them asked.

"She's not from here," said another, with a voice like a distant chime.

Lily smiled nervously, unsure of what to say. But before she could speak, a particularly grand figure floated toward her. This Cloud Person was taller than

"

the others, with a crown made of golden sunlight and a flowing robe that seemed to be woven from the rays of the setting sun. His wings were larger and more ornate, and they shimmered with all the colors of the rainbow.

"Welcome to the Cloud Kingdom, young traveler," the grand figure said in a voice that was both commanding and kind. "I am Cirrus, King of the Clouds. We do not often have visitors from the world below."

Lily's eyes widened in awe. "Your Majesty," she stammered, "I—I did not mean to intrude. I was just... well, I was just blowing a bubble, and it brought me here."

King Cirrus smiled, his eyes twinkling like the stars in a midnight sky. "Ah, the bubblegum balloon. It is a rare and magical thing, indeed. Only those with a brave heart and a curious spirit can be carried by it to our kingdom."

Lily felt a warm glow of pride at the king's words. "This place is amazing," she said, looking around in wonder. "I've never seen anything like it."

King Cirrus nodded. "The Cloud Kingdom is a place of dreams and imagination, a world that exists just beyond the reach of those who do not believe in magic. But for you, young one, the journey has just begun. Come, let us show you the wonders of our realm."

With a wave of his hand, King Cirrus gestured for Lily to follow. The other Cloud People parted to make way, their wings fluttering softly as they hovered nearby. Lily walked beside the king, feeling as though she were in a dream.

The Cloud Kingdom was more beautiful than anything Lily could have imagined. The castle itself was made of swirling clouds, with towers that seemed to stretch endlessly into the sky. The walls were adorned with patterns of light and shadow, constantly shifting, and changing like the colors of a sunset. Every now and then, a soft breeze would pass through, causing the entire structure to shimmer and ripple.

As they walked, King Cirrus pointed out various parts of the kingdom. "Over there is the Cloud Garden," he said, gesturing toward a vast expanse filled with blooming flowers made entirely of mist. The flowers swayed gently in the breeze, their petals glowing in shades of pink, purple, and blue.

Lily gasped in delight. "They're beautiful!"

"They are the dreams of the world below," King Cirrus explained. "Every time someone on Earth dreams of something wonderful, it takes the form of a flower here in our garden. We take care of them until the dreamer wakes, and then the flowers fade back into the mist."

Lily marveled at the idea that the flowers she was seeing were the dreams of people just like her. She could not help but wonder if one of them might be her own dream, captured in the Cloud Garden.

They continued, passing through archways made of rainbows and across bridges that shimmered with the colors of the aurora borealis. The Cloud People followed them, their soft laughter filling the air like the tinkling of wind chimes. Everywhere she looked, Lily saw something new and magical—cloud sculptures that changed shape with the wind, fountains that flowed with liquid light, and birds made of mist that sang songs she had never heard before.

Eventually, they reached the center of the kingdom, where a grand courtyard opened before them. In the middle of the courtyard stood a magnificent tree, its branches spreading wide and high. The tree was made of pure, glowing light, and its leaves were delicate wisps of cloud that sparkled with every color of the rainbow.

"This is the Heart of the Kingdom," King Cirrus said, his voice full of reverence. "It is the source of all the magic in our world. As long as the Heart of the Kingdom remains strong, the Cloud Kingdom will thrive."

Lily stared in awe at the tree, feeling the magic radiating from it. It was a feeling of warmth, comfort, and joy all rolled into one. She could sense the connection between this magical world and the world below, and she realized that this place reflected all the good and beautiful things in the world.

"Thank you for bringing me here," Lily said softly, turning to King Cirrus. "This is the most amazing adventure I've ever had."

The king smiled gently. "Your adventure is far from over, Lily. The bubblegum balloon has brought you here for a reason. There is something special waiting for you, something only you can discover."

Lily's heart fluttered with anticipation. "What is it?" she asked eagerly.

King Cirrus shook his head. "That is for you to find out. But remember this, young traveler: the magic of the Cloud Kingdom is not just in the clouds, but in your heart as well. Trust in yourself, and you will find your way."

Lily nodded, feeling a surge of determination. She did not know what awaited her, but she was ready to face whatever challenges came her way. She had the magic of the Cloud Kingdom and the guidance of the pink balloon to help her.

As she stood in the courtyard, surrounded by the beauty, and wonder of the Cloud Kingdom, Lily felt a sense of purpose. This was more than just an adventure—it was a journey of discovery, not just of this magical world, but of herself as well.

And so, with the pink balloon floating by her side and the words of King Cirrus echoing in her heart, Lily set off to explore the Cloud Kingdom, eager to uncover the secrets it held.

Chapter 4: The Secret of the Cloud Garden

Lily's heart raced with excitement as she ventured deeper into the Cloud Kingdom, her pink balloon floating gently beside her. King Cirrus had hinted that something special was waiting for her, and she was determined to find it. The Cloud People continued to flutter around her, their soft whispers of encouragement filling the air like a chorus of tiny bells.

As she wandered through the ethereal streets, she found herself drawn back to the Cloud Garden. The garden had captured her imagination with its shimmering, dreamlike flowers, and she could not shake the feeling that it held a secret—one that might be the key to her adventure.

The garden was even more beautiful up close. Each flower seemed to glow with its own inner light, casting a soft, colorful glow across the misty ground. The petals were delicate and translucent, like the wings of butterflies, and they swayed gently in the breeze, as if dancing to a silent melody.

Lily knelt beside a particularly vibrant flower, its petals a deep shade of violet with streaks of gold. She reached out to touch it, and as her fingers brushed against the soft petals, she felt a warmth spread through her. It was a comforting, familiar feeling, like the warmth of her mother's embrace or the coziness of her favorite blanket on a cold night.

"Each flower is a dream," she murmured to herself, remembering King Cirrus's words. "But what kind of dream is this?"

As she pondered this, a soft voice interrupted her thoughts. "You have a gentle touch, young one."

Lily looked up, startled, and saw an elderly Cloud Woman standing beside her. She was small and frail-looking, with hair as white as snow and eyes that twinkled with the wisdom of ages. She wore a simple robe made of mist, and her wings fluttered gently as she moved.

"Who are you?" Lily asked, her curiosity piqued.

"I am Nimbus, the Keeper of the Garden," the old woman replied with a kind smile. "I tend to the dreams that grow here and ensure they flourish until their time comes."

Lily stood up and dusted off her dress. "It's so beautiful here," she said, looking around in awe. "But I feel like there's something more—something I'm supposed to find."

Nimbus's smile deepened, and she nodded knowingly. "You are very perceptive, child. The Cloud Garden holds many secrets, some of which are meant only for those with open hearts and curious minds. Perhaps the garden has something to reveal to you."

Lily's heart skipped a beat. "How do I find it?"

Nimbus stepped closer to her, her voice dropping to a whisper. "To find the secret of the Cloud Garden, you must first listen to the dreams. Each flower here is a dream waiting to be heard. Close your eyes, and let the garden speak to you."

Lily did as she was told, closing her eyes, and taking a deep breath. She stood still, allowing the soft breeze to wash over her, carrying with it the faint, melodic hum of the garden. At first, she heard nothing but the gentle rustling of leaves and the distant murmur of the Cloud People. But as she focused more intently, she began to hear something else—a faint, musical tune, like the tinkling of a wind chime.

The melody grew clearer, and Lily realized it was coming from the flowers themselves. Each one seemed to sing its own song, a soft, sweet lullaby that filled the air with magic. She listened closely, letting the music guide her. Slowly, she turned in the direction of the strongest melody, following it deeper into the garden.

With each step, the song grew louder, until it became a chorus of voices, all harmonizing together. Lily opened her eyes, and to her astonishment, she saw that the flowers were glowing more brightly than ever, their colors more vibrant, their light more intense. It was as if the garden was alive, responding to her presence.

She walked until she reached a small, secluded clearing in the heart of the garden. Here, the flowers were larger and more radiant than any she had seen before. In the center of the clearing stood a single, magnificent flower, unlike any other. Its petals were a brilliant shade of pink, and it glowed with a light that seemed to pulse like a heartbeat.

Lily approached the flower, her breath catching in her throat. There was something incredibly special about this flower—something that called to her in a way she could not explain. She reached out to touch it, and as her fingers brushed against the petals, she felt a rush of warmth and energy, as if the flower were alive and welcoming her.

Nimbus appeared beside her once more, her eyes twinkling with a knowing smile. "This is the Heart Flower," she said softly. "It is the heart of the Cloud Garden, and it contains the dreams of the entire kingdom. Only those who are truly meant to find it are drawn here."

Lily gazed at the Heart Flower in wonder. "What does it mean?"

"The Heart Flower has the power to grant a wish," Nimbus explained. "But not just any wish—only the purest, most selfless wish will be granted. The flower responds to the deepest desires of the heart, and it has chosen you, Lily, to make that wish."

Lily's mind raced. A wish? What should she wish for? There were so many things she could ask for—a lifetime supply of bubblegum, the ability to fly, or even the chance to stay in the Cloud Kingdom forever. But as she looked at the Heart Flower, she knew that those wishes were not what the flower was asking for.

Instead, Lily thought about her family, her friends, and her home. She thought about all the people she cared about and what might bring them happiness. And then, deep in her heart, she knew what she had to wish for.

She closed her eyes, placed her hands gently on the Heart Flower, and whispered her wish.

"I wish," she said softly, "for everyone I care about to find their own happiness, whatever that may be."

The moment the words left her lips, the Heart Flower began to glow even more brightly. The light pulsed with a warm, golden hue, filling the entire clearing with a gentle radiance. Lily felt a wave of peace and contentment wash over her, as if the flower had heard her wish and was granting it with all the magic it possessed.

Nimbus smiled at Lily; her eyes filled with pride. "You have a kind heart, Lily. Your wish will bring joy to many, and the Cloud Kingdom will always remember the day you touched the Heart Flower."

Lily smiled back, feeling a deep sense of fulfillment. She knew that her wish would come true, and that the people she loved would find their own paths to happiness.

As the light from the Heart Flower slowly faded, Lily felt a gentle tug on her hand. She looked down and saw the pink balloon hovering beside her, as if ready to take her on the next leg of her adventure.

Nimbus nodded toward the balloon. "Your journey is not over yet, young one. The Cloud Kingdom has many more wonders to show you. But remember, the magic of the Heart Flower will always be with you, no matter where you go."

Lily nodded, her heart swelling with gratitude. She gave Nimbus a hug, thanking her for guiding her to the Heart Flower, and then turned to the pink balloon.

With a final look at the beautiful Cloud Garden, Lily climbed onto the balloon, ready for whatever lay ahead. The balloon began to rise, lifting her gently into the air once more. As she floated away, Lily looked back and saw the Heart Flower glowing softly in the distance, a beacon of hope and magic in the heart of the Cloud Kingdom.

And so, with the wind in her hair and the magic of the Heart Flower in her heart, Lily continued her journey through the Cloud Kingdom, eager to see what new adventures awaited her.

Chapter 5: The Stormy Challenge

Lily floated higher and higher, the pink balloon carrying her above the Cloud Garden and into the vast expanse of the Cloud Kingdom. The gentle breeze that had guided her earlier began to shift, becoming stronger and more unpredictable. She clung to the balloon, her heart pounding with a mix of excitement and trepidation. The sky around her started to darken, and she could see thick, gray clouds gathering on the horizon.

The Cloud Kingdom, so peaceful and serene just moments ago, was beginning to change. The air grew colder, and the once soft and fluffy clouds turned dark and menacing. Thunder rumbled in the distance, and flashes of lightning lit up the sky. Lily's grip on the balloon tightened as she realized that she was heading straight into a storm.

The wind picked up, buffeting her back and forth as the balloon struggled to stay on course. The storm clouds loomed closer, swirling ominously, and crackling with energy. Lily had never seen a storm like this before—it was powerful and wild, a force of nature that seemed almost alive.

As she approached the storm, a voice called out to her through the howling wind. "Lily! Beware of the Tempest King!"

Lily looked around, trying to find the source of the voice, but all she could see were the storm clouds swirling around her. The voice sounded familiar, though, like an echo of something she had heard before. It was full of warning, urging her to be careful.

Just then, the storm clouds parted, and a massive figure emerged from the swirling mist. It was a towering, menacing being made entirely of storm clouds, with eyes that glowed like lightning and a voice that boomed like thunder. He was wrapped in a cloak of swirling wind, and his presence commanded the sky.

"I am the Tempest King!" the figure roared, his voice shaking the very air around him. "No one passes through my domain without facing my challenge!"

Lily's heart raced as she stared up at the Tempest King. He was the embodiment of the storm, a powerful and fearsome ruler of the skies. But she knew she could not turn back now—her journey through the Cloud Kingdom had led her here, and she had to face whatever challenge the Tempest King had in store.

"What is your challenge, Tempest King?" Lily called out, trying to keep her voice steady.

The Tempest King's eyes narrowed as he studied her, and the storm around them seemed to grow even more intense. "You are brave, little one," he said, his voice rumbling like distant thunder. "But bravery alone will not be enough to conquer the storm. You must prove your worth by passing through the heart of the tempest. Only then will you be allowed to continue your journey."

Lily's eyes widened. The heart of the tempest? That sounded terrifying! But she knew she could not back down now. She had come this far, and she was not about to let fear stop her from completing her adventure.

"I accept your challenge," Lily declared, her voice strong and determined.

The Tempest King nodded, a faint smile playing on his lips. "Very well, young one. But beware—the storm will test you in ways you cannot imagine. Hold on to your courage, and trust in the magic of the Cloud Kingdom."

With that, the Tempest King raised his arms, and the storm clouds swirled even faster, forming a massive vortex that stretched high into the sky. The wind howled and roared, and lightning crackled all around Lily as the balloon was pulled toward the center of the tempest.

Lily held on tightly, her heart pounding in her chest. The balloon was tossed and turned by the raging winds, spinning her around in a dizzying whirl of dark clouds and flashes of light. She could barely see anything through the storm, and the noise was deafening, like a thousand drums beating in unison.

But through it all, Lily kept the Tempest King's words in her mind: *Hold on to your courage, and trust in the magic of the Cloud Kingdom.* She focused on staying calm, knowing that the magic of the Heart Flower was with her, guiding her through the storm.

As the balloon was pulled deeper into the heart of the tempest, Lily felt the storm's power growing even stronger. The winds whipped around her like a tornado, and the lightning flashed so brightly that it hurt her eyes. But instead of giving in to fear, she closed her eyes and focused on the warmth of the Heart Flower's magic. She could feel it pulsing gently in her chest, a steady rhythm that reminded her of her wish for happiness and the strength it had given her.

The storm raged on, but Lily's fear began to fade. She realized that the tempest, as terrifying as it was, was a part of the Cloud Kingdom—a place of magic and wonder. The Tempest King was not trying to hurt her; he was testing her, challenging her to prove her courage and determination.

With this new understanding, Lily opened her eyes and investigated the heart of the storm. The swirling winds and flashing lightning did not seem as frightening anymore. Instead, she saw them as part of the Cloud Kingdom's wild beauty—a powerful force of nature that she could face with confidence.

Lily took a deep breath, then called out to the Tempest King. "I am not afraid anymore! I trust in the magic of the Cloud Kingdom, and I am ready to face your challenge!"

The Tempest King's eyes widened in surprise, and the storm around them began to calm. The winds slowed, and the lightning dimmed, leaving only a soft rumble of thunder in the distance. The Tempest King looked at Lily with a newfound respect.

"You have passed the test, Lily," the Tempest King said, his voice no longer booming with thunder but filled with admiration. "You have shown great courage and wisdom in facing the storm. You are worthy to continue your journey."

Lily smiled, feeling a rush of relief and pride. She had done it! She had faced the storm and come out stronger on the other side.

The Tempest King raised his hand, and the storm clouds parted, revealing a clear path through the sky. The pink balloon floated gently beside Lily, ready to carry her onward.

"Remember, young one," the Tempest King said as Lily prepared to leave, "the strength you found in the storm is always within you. No matter what challenges you face, trust in yourself and the magic that surrounds you."

Lily nodded, feeling a deep sense of gratitude. "Thank you, Tempest King," she said. "I'll never forget this."

With a final nod, the Tempest King faded back into the storm clouds, leaving Lily alone in the calm, open sky. The pink balloon began to rise once more, carrying her away from the tempest and toward the next adventure that awaited her in the Cloud Kingdom.

As she floated away, Lily looked back at the storm, now just a distant rumble on the horizon. She knew that whatever lay ahead, she was ready for it. The magic of the Cloud Kingdom was with her, and she had proven to herself that she could face any challenge with courage and determination.

And so, with the wind at her back and the sky clear before her, Lily continued her journey through the Cloud Kingdom, eager to discover what other wonders and challenges awaited her.

Chapter 6: The Rainbow Bridge

As Lily soared away from the tempest, the sky began to transform. The dark storm clouds gradually gave way to a clear, azure expanse, and the air grew warmer and more inviting. The gentle breeze carried with it the scent of something sweet, like fresh flowers after a summer rain. Lily felt a sense of peace wash over her, and the pink balloon floated serenely, as if it too were enjoying the calm after the storm.

She looked around, taking in the beauty of the Cloud Kingdom. The white, fluffy clouds beneath her shimmered in the sunlight, and in the distance, she could see something breathtaking—a shimmering, multicolored arch stretching across the sky. It was a rainbow, more vibrant and dazzling than any she had ever seen on Earth. It seemed to pulse with energy, radiating colors that danced and shifted with every moment.

Lily's eyes widened in awe as she realized that this was no ordinary rainbow. It was enormous, spanning the entire horizon, and as the balloon drifted closer, she could see that the rainbow was not just a simple arc of color. It was a bridge, made of shimmering, translucent light that connected one side of the sky to the other.

"The Rainbow Bridge," Lily whispered to herself, feeling a surge of excitement. She had heard stories of magical bridges that connected different realms, and she wondered where this one might lead. The pink balloon seemed to sense her curiosity, gently guiding her toward the bridge.

As she approached, Lily noticed that the colors of the rainbow were even more magnificent up close. Each hue glowed with a vibrant, otherworldly light, and she could see tiny sparkles of magic dancing within the bands of color. The bridge looked solid enough to walk on, yet it shimmered like a mirage, as if it were made of pure light and magic.

Lily's heart raced with anticipation. She was not sure what awaited her on the other side of the bridge, but she knew she had to cross it. With a deep breath, she climbed off the balloon and stepped onto the Rainbow Bridge.

The moment her foot touched the bridge, she felt a tingle of energy run through her. The surface was smooth and cool beneath her feet, yet it seemed to hum with life, as if the bridge itself were aware of her presence. The colors shifted and swirled around her, creating a dazzling display of light that filled her with wonder.

With the pink balloon floating beside her, Lily began to walk across the Rainbow Bridge. Each step she took felt light and effortless, as if the bridge were lifting her up and carrying her forward. The colors around her swirled and danced, forming patterns and shapes that seemed almost alive. She could hear a soft, melodic tune playing in the distance, like the music of the stars.

As she continued, Lily noticed that the bridge was not just a path—it was an experience, a journey through a world of pure magic. The colors around her began to take on forms, creating images and scenes that seemed to tell a story. She saw visions of lush green meadows, sparkling rivers, and towering mountains, all bathed in the light of a golden sun. She saw creatures of all kinds—animals, birds, and even fantastical beings—living in harmony within this radiant world.

The further she walked, the more the scenes began to change. The images became more abstract, showing swirling galaxies, stars being born, and worlds beyond her imagination. It was as if the Rainbow Bridge was revealing the secrets of the universe, showing her the infinite possibilities of magic and wonder that existed in the Cloud Kingdom.

Lily was entranced by the beauty of it all. She felt as though she were walking through a dream, one that was both real and unreal at the same time. The bridge seemed to stretch on forever, carrying her deeper into the heart of the Cloud Kingdom.

But as she continued, Lily noticed something strange. The colors of the rainbow, once so vibrant and clear, started to fade. The scenes around her grew dim, and the once-bright light began to flicker. A sense of unease crept into her heart, and she wondered if something was wrong.

The pink balloon tugged gently at her hand, urging her to keep going. Lily hesitated, but she trusted the balloon and pressed on. The further she walked, the more the colors faded, until the bridge itself seemed to be losing its light.

Finally, she reached the center of the Rainbow Bridge, and there she found the source of the dimming light. A small, sad figure was sitting in the middle of the bridge, its head bowed and its body curled up in a ball. It was a creature made entirely of light, with a shimmering, translucent form that glowed faintly with the colors of the rainbow. But the light was dim, as if it were fading away.

Lily's heart went out to the creature. It looked so lonely and fragile, as if it were losing its strength. She kneeled beside it and gently placed a hand on its shoulder.

"Hello," Lily said softly. "Are you okay?"

The creature looked up at her, its eyes filled with sadness. "I am the Rainbow Keeper," it said in a voice that was barely more than a whisper. "I guard the Rainbow Bridge and ensure its light shines brightly for all who cross it. But I am afraid... I am losing my power."

Lily's eyes widened in concern. "Why are you losing your power? What can I do to help?"

The Rainbow Keeper sighed, its light flickering. "The light of the Rainbow Bridge comes from the hopes and dreams of those who walk upon it. But lately, fewer, and fewer travelers have crossed the bridge, and those who do bring with them fear and doubt instead of hope. The light of the bridge is fading, and so am I."

Lily felt a pang of sadness. The Rainbow Bridge was such a beautiful and magical place, and it broke her heart to think that it was fading away. But she also felt a spark of determination. She knew she had to do something to help the Rainbow Keeper and restore the bridge's light.

"Maybe I can help," Lily said, her voice filled with resolve. "I believe in the magic of the Cloud Kingdom, and I know that hope and dreams are stronger than fear. If I can bring hope back to the bridge, will that restore its light?"

The Rainbow Keeper looked at her with a glimmer of hope in its eyes. "Perhaps," it said softly. "But it will not be easy. You must find a way to rekindle the light within the hearts of those who cross the bridge. Only then will the Rainbow Bridge shine as brightly as it once did."

Lily nodded, determination filling her heart. "I will do it. I will find a way to bring hope back to the bridge."

The Rainbow Keeper gave her a small, grateful smile. "Thank you, Lily. You have a kind and courageous heart. I believe you can do it."

With renewed purpose, Lily stood up and looked around. The bridge was still dim, but she could feel the faint pulse of magic within it, waiting to be awakened. She knew that she needed to inspire others to believe in the magic of the Cloud Kingdom, just as she did.

The pink balloon floated beside her, its light brightening as if sensing her resolve. Lily took a deep breath and began to walk back along the bridge, determined to restore its light.

As she walked, she thought about all the wonders she had seen in the Cloud Kingdom—the Cloud Garden, the Tempest King, and now the Rainbow Bridge. Each of them was a part of a magical world that existed beyond the ordinary, a world where anything was possible if you just believed.

Lily knew that the key to restoring the bridge's light was to share that belief with others. She needed to help them see the magic that she saw, to help them find the hope and wonder in their own hearts.

With that thought in mind, Lily began to hum a tune, a soft, melodic song that carried on the breeze. It was a song of hope, of dreams, and of the magic that existed within every heart. As she hummed, she felt the bridge beneath her begin to respond, its colors brightening ever so slightly.

The further she walked, the louder her song became, until she was singing with all her heart. The words flowed from her lips like a river of light, filling the air with warmth and joy. She sang of the wonders of the Cloud Kingdom, of the beauty of the Rainbow Bridge, and of the power of hope and dreams.

And as she sang, the light of the bridge began to return. The colors grew brighter and more vibrant, and the scenes of magic and wonder began to reappear. The Rainbow Keeper, watching from the center of the bridge, felt its strength returning, its light shining brighter with every note of Lily's song.

By the time Lily reached the end of the Rainbow Bridge, it was glowing with all the colors of the rainbow, a dazzling display of light and magic that stretched across the sky. The Rainbow Keeper stood tall and strong once more, its form shining brightly with the restored light of the bridge.

"Thank you, Lily," the Rainbow Keeper called out, its voice now filled with joy. "You have restored the Rainbow Bridge, and with it, the hope, and dreams of all who cross it. The Cloud Kingdom is grateful for your courage and your kindness."

Lily smiled, feeling a deep sense of accomplishment. She had done it—she had brought hope back to the Rainbow Bridge, and in doing so, she had saved a part of the magical world she had come to love.

The pink balloon floated beside her, glowing with the colors of the rainbow, as if celebrating their victory. With the Rainbow Keeper's blessing, Lily climbed back onto the balloon, ready to continue her journey through the Cloud Kingdom. As the balloon rose into the sky, Lily looked back at the Rainbow Bridge, now shining brightly and beautifully. She knew that whatever lay ahead, she would face it with hope and determination, guided by the magic of the Cloud Kingdom and the lessons she had learned along the way.

And so, with the wind at her back and the light of the Rainbow Bridge shining in her heart, Lily continued her adventure, eager to discover the next wonder that awaited her in the magical realm above the clouds.

Chapter 7: The Enchanted Forest

As the pink balloon drifted away from the now resplendent Rainbow Bridge, Lily marveled at the view below. The sky was clear and the sunlight bathed the world in a warm, golden hue. The clouds parted to reveal a lush, green landscape stretching out beneath her. Lily could see towering trees, sparkling streams, and vibrant meadows—all bathed in the soft light of the Cloud Kingdom.

The balloon floated lower, gradually descending toward a dense, mystical forest that seemed to shimmer with its own magical aura. The trees were tall and majestic, their leaves a mix of vivid greens and sparkling golds. It was as if the entire forest was alive with enchantment. Lily felt a thrill of excitement as the balloon approached the edge of the forest.

As they descended, she saw that the forest was more than just a collection of trees. The trunks were adorned with intricate patterns of light, and the underbrush was filled with glowing flowers and plants. Tiny, fairy-like creatures flitted between the branches, their wings leaving trails of sparkling dust in the air.

The pink balloon gently touched down on a soft, moss-covered clearing at the edge of the Enchanted Forest. Lily stepped out, her feet sinking slightly into the plush, verdant ground. The air was filled with the sweet scent of blooming flowers and the melodious songs of hidden creatures.

As she stood there, taking in the beauty of the forest, a soft voice spoke from behind her. "Welcome to the Enchanted Forest, traveler."

Lily turned to see a graceful figure stepping out from among the trees. It was a tall, elegant woman dressed in flowing robes that shimmered with the colors of the forest. Her hair was a cascade of silver, and her eyes sparkled with a deep, knowing light. She moved with a fluid grace, as if she were part of the very magic of the forest.

"I am Elara, the Guardian of the Enchanted Forest," the woman said with a warm smile. "I have been expecting you."

Lily's eyes widened with curiosity. "You have been expecting me? How?"

Elara's smile widened. "The magic of the Cloud Kingdom is intertwined with the magic of the Enchanted Forest. I knew that a brave and kind-hearted traveler would soon arrive. The forest has sensed your presence and is eager to share its secrets with you."

Lily felt a rush of excitement. "I would love to learn more about the forest. What is it that I need to know?"

Elara's eyes twinkled with a hint of mischief. "The Enchanted Forest is a place of wonder and mystery. It holds many secrets and challenges, each designed to test the heart and spirit of those who enter. To truly understand the magic of the forest, you must embark on a quest."

"A quest?" Lily asked, intrigued. "What kind of quest?"

Elara gestured toward the heart of the forest, where the trees formed a natural archway. "Deep within the forest lies a hidden glade, where the ancient Tree of Light stands. It is said that the Tree of Light holds the wisdom and magic of the entire forest. However, it is protected by a series of trials that test the courage, kindness, and wisdom of those who seek it."

Lily's heart leaped with excitement. She had faced challenges before, but this sounded like a true adventure. "I will do it. I will find the Tree of Light and complete the trials."

Elara nodded approvingly. "Very well. Remember, the trials are not just physical tests; they are meant to challenge your inner strength and the purity of your heart. Approach each trial with an open mind and a compassionate spirit."

With that, Elara stepped aside, and Lily began her journey into the Enchanted Forest. The trees closed in around her, their branches forming a natural canopy that filtered the sunlight into a soft, dappled glow. The air was cool and refreshing, and the sounds of the forest—rustling leaves, chirping birds, and the occasional distant roar of a magical creature—created a soothing, rhythmic background.

As Lily walked deeper into the forest, she came across the first of the trials: a wide, shimmering river that flowed through the heart of the woods. The water was crystal clear, and its surface sparkled with a myriad of colors. On the other side of the river, she could see a path leading further into the forest, but there was no bridge or obvious way to cross.

Lily approached the river, studying it carefully. She noticed that the water was filled with floating, luminous stones that glowed gently. They formed a natural pathway across the river, but they were spaced quite far apart, making it difficult to cross.

Just then, a soft voice spoke from the riverbank. "To cross the river, you must find the right path."

Lily looked around and saw a small, golden fish swimming near the edge of the river. It had delicate fins that sparkled like diamonds and eyes that seemed to hold a world of secrets.

"Hello," Lily said softly. "Can you help me find the way across?"

The golden fish swam closer, its eyes filled with a knowing glint. "To find the right path, you must trust in your heart and listen to the magic of the river. Follow the stones that shine the brightest, and you will reach the other side."

With that advice in mind, Lily took a deep breath and stepped onto the first glowing stone. It was smooth and cool beneath her feet, and it seemed to pulse gently with light. She carefully stepped onto the next stone, choosing the one that shone the brightest. Each step she took was guided by the light of the stones, and she moved with careful precision.

As she crossed the river, Lily felt a sense of calm and focus. She trusted in the magic of the forest and the guidance of the golden fish. The journey across the river was a delicate balance of courage and trust, and she made it to the other side without incident.

When she reached the far bank, the path continued through the forest, leading her toward the heart of the woods. The trees seemed to part before her, creating a natural pathway that guided her deeper into the Enchanted Forest.

The next trial awaited her: a grove filled with a dense, swirling mist. The mist was thick and almost tangible, and it obscured her view of what lay ahead. Lily could sense that the mist was hiding something important, but she could not see through it.

Taking a deep breath, Lily stepped into the mist. The air was cool and damp, and the mist swirled around her, creating eerie shapes and patterns. It was difficult to see or hear anything clearly, and Lily felt a pang of uncertainty. But she remembered Elara's words: the trials were meant to test her inner strength and purity of heart.

With determination, she pressed on through the mist. She focused on the warmth of the Heart Flower's magic and the hope that had guided her so far. The mist seemed to part slightly, revealing faint glimpses of the path ahead. Lily followed these glimpses, trusting her instincts and the magic of the forest.

After what felt like hours, the mist began to thin, and Lily emerged into a beautiful glade. The glade was bathed in a soft, golden light, and in the center stood a majestic tree with silver leaves and a trunk that seemed to glow with an inner light. It was the Tree of Light, exactly as Elara had described.

Lily approached the Tree of Light, feeling a sense of awe and reverence. The tree was magnificent, its branches stretching high into the sky and its roots forming a network of intricate patterns on the ground. The light that emanated from the tree was warm and soothing, and Lily could feel its magic filling the glade.

As she stood before the Tree of Light, a voice spoke softly from within the tree. "You have completed the trials and shown great courage and kindness. The magic of the Enchanted Forest is now yours to discover."

Lily looked around the glade, feeling a deep sense of fulfillment. She had faced the trials and proved her worth, and now she was ready to learn the secrets of the Tree of Light.

With a heart full of gratitude, she touched the tree's trunk and felt a surge of magic flow through her. The Tree of Light had granted her the wisdom and strength she needed for the rest of her journey.

As she prepared to leave the glade, she knew that the Enchanted Forest had shared its magic with her, and she was ready to continue her adventure. The pink balloon waited patiently at the edge of the glade, ready to carry her onward to the next chapter of her journey through the Cloud Kingdom.

Chapter 8: The Whispering Caves

With the wisdom and magic of the Tree of Light filling her heart, Lily climbed back into the pink balloon, which gently lifted her into the sky. As she floated away from the Enchanted Forest, she gazed down at the lush, green landscape now fading into the distance. The sky was clear, and the warm light of the Cloud Kingdom enveloped her in a comforting embrace.

The balloon carried her over rolling hills and sparkling rivers until it reached a series of towering mountain peaks, their craggy tops reaching up to touch the sky. Nestled among these mountains were a series of dark, mysterious caves. The entrance to each cave was framed by shimmering crystals that glowed softly in the twilight.

As the balloon descended toward the caves, Lily felt a sense of anticipation. The caves seemed to hum with a quiet, mystical energy, and she could hear faint echoes of whispers carried on the wind. She carefully guided the balloon to a smooth, rocky platform near the entrance of the largest cave.

Stepping out of the balloon, Lily approached the cave entrance. The whispers grew louder, and she could make out fragments of words, though they were too faint to understand clearly. The air around the cave was cool and still, and the faint glow of the crystals cast an eerie light on the cave walls.

Taking a deep breath, Lily entered the cave. The interior was dimly lit by the crystals embedded in the walls, casting shimmering reflections on the cavernous space. The whispers seemed to grow stronger as she ventured deeper into the cave, echoing off the walls in a haunting, melodic chorus.

As she walked, the cave seemed to shift and change, with passages leading off in various directions. It was easy to become disoriented in the twisting labyrinth, but Lily remained focused, guided by the whispers that seemed to call her forward. She felt a sense of purpose and determination, knowing that the Whispering Caves held important lessons and challenges for her.

Eventually, she came upon a large, circular chamber. The ceiling of the chamber was high, and the walls were adorned with glittering, ancient runes. In the center of the chamber was a pedestal, and upon it rested a small, ornate box. The whispers grew louder, forming a coherent, rhythmic chant that seemed to emanate from the box.

Lily approached the pedestal and examined the box. It was intricately carved with symbols and patterns that seemed to shift and change as she looked at them. The whispers were now clear and distinct, though the words were still difficult to understand.

"Open the box," the whispers urged. "Find the key to the next trial."

Lily hesitated for a moment, feeling a twinge of uncertainty. The box was beautifully crafted, but she wondered what lay inside. With a deep breath, she carefully lifted the lid of the box.

Inside, she found a delicate, silver key resting on a bed of velvet. The key was adorned with intricate designs that matched the runes on the cave walls. As she held it in her hand, the whispers grew softer, almost as if they were guiding her to the next step.

The chamber began to shift, and a new passageway revealed itself, leading deeper into the cave. Lily knew that the key was important, and she followed the passageway with a sense of purpose.

The path led her to another chamber, this one filled with a series of shimmering, floating platforms. The platforms hovered in mid-air, each one glowing with a soft, ethereal light. The room was filled with the same whispers, now forming a more urgent and rhythmic chant.

Lily realized that she needed to use the key to unlock the next part of her journey. She looked around and saw a large, ornate door at the far end of the chamber, its surface covered with intricate patterns that matched those on the key. The whispers seemed to be guiding her toward the door.

She approached the door and inserted the key into the lock. The key turned smoothly, and the door creaked open, revealing a new passageway bathed in a soft, golden light. The whispers grew louder and more celebratory, as if acknowledging her success.

With the door open, Lily stepped through the passageway and into a large, beautifully lit cavern. The light in this cavern was warm and golden, and the walls were adorned with shimmering, colorful crystals. In the center of the cavern was a pool of clear, sparkling water. The surface of the pool was calm and mirror-like, reflecting the light and creating a sense of serenity.

At the edge of the pool stood a figure—a wise, ancient-looking creature with a long, flowing beard and kind, knowing eyes. The creature was a guardian of the cave, and its presence radiated a sense of peace and wisdom.

"Welcome, Lily," the guardian said in a deep, melodic voice. "You have successfully navigated the Whispering Caves and completed the trials within. You have shown great courage, wisdom, and perseverance."

Lily felt a sense of accomplishment and relief. "Thank you. The journey through the caves has been challenging, but I have learned a lot from it."

The guardian smiled. "The Whispering Caves test the heart and spirit of those who enter. They reveal truths about oneself and teach valuable lessons. You have passed the trials with grace and integrity."

The guardian gestured toward the pool. "Look into the waters of the pool, and you will see a vision of what lies ahead in your journey."

Lily approached the pool and gazed into its clear, reflective surface. As she looked, the water began to swirl and shift, forming images and scenes that unfolded before her eyes. She saw glimpses of the Cloud Kingdom, its magical landscapes, and inhabitants, and she glimpsed future challenges and adventures that awaited her.

The visions showed her the path she needed to follow, guiding her toward the next stage of her journey. The images were both beautiful and inspiring, filled with hope and wonder.

As the visions faded, the guardian spoke again. "Remember the lessons you have learned in the Whispering Caves. Trust in yourself, follow your heart, and the magic of the Cloud Kingdom will guide you."

Lily nodded, feeling a deep sense of gratitude. "Thank you for your guidance and wisdom."

With that, she bid farewell to the guardian and made her way back through the cavern and the Whispering Caves. The path had been challenging, but she felt stronger and more confident as she emerged from the cave and returned to the pink balloon.

As she prepared to continue her journey, she looked back at the Whispering Caves with a sense of accomplishment. The caves had tested her in many ways, but they had also given her valuable insights and guidance for the adventures that lay ahead.

With the pink balloon ready to carry her onward, Lily set her sights on the horizon, eager to discover the next wonder and challenge in the Cloud Kingdom. The magic of the Whispering Caves was now a part of her, and she was ready to face whatever came next with courage and hope.

Chapter 9: The Floating Gardens

The pink balloon floated gently through the sky, carried by a soft breeze as Lily ventured away from the Whispering Caves. The golden light of the Cloud Kingdom bathed the landscape in a warm, serene glow. As she drifted onward, Lily could not help but feel a sense of excitement for the next chapter of her adventure.

Below, she saw a mesmerizing sight—an expanse of lush, vibrant gardens suspended in mid-air. Floating islands, each adorned with vibrant flowers and greenery, drifted gently through the sky like a colorful patchwork quilt. Cascading waterfalls flowed from one floating island to another, creating a network of sparkling rivers that shimmered in the sunlight.

The balloon descended towards the gardens, and Lily marveled at the beauty of the floating islands. Each island was unique, with lush trees, blooming flowers, and winding paths. Some islands had whimsical, fairy-tale cottages, while others were home to colorful, fantastical creatures. The air was filled with the sweet fragrance of blooming flowers and the gentle hum of magic.

The balloon landed softly on a grassy island with a beautiful view of the surrounding gardens. Lily stepped out and took a deep breath, inhaling the fresh, floral scent. The island she had landed on was adorned with vibrant, multicolored flowers and an array of fascinating plants. A delicate, winding path led through the garden, inviting her to explore.

As she began to walk along the path, she encountered a cheerful, talking flower with bright, smiling petals. The flower's voice was gentle and melodious, and it greeted her with a warm, friendly tone.

"Welcome to the Floating Gardens!" the flower said. "I'm Petal, and I'm here to guide you through our magical realm."

Lily smiled at the talking flower. "Thank you, Petal. This place is incredible. Can you tell me more about the Floating Gardens?"

Petal swayed slightly in the breeze, its petals fluttering with joy. "The Floating Gardens are a realm of magic and harmony. Each island is unique, and they all work together to maintain the balance and beauty of our world. However, our magic has been disturbed recently, and we need your help to restore it."

Lily's curiosity was piqued. "What kind of help do you need?"

Petal's expression became more serious. "There is an ancient garden at the heart of the Floating Gardens, known as the Heart of the Garden. It holds the essence of our magic and ensures that all the floating islands remain in harmony. But recently, the Heart of the Garden has lost its power, and the islands have begun to drift apart. We need someone with a pure heart and a strong spirit to help restore its magic."

Lily nodded, feeling a sense of determination. "I would be happy to help. How can I reach the Heart of the Garden?"

Petal pointed toward a distant island, one that was larger and more radiant than the others. "The Heart of the Garden lies on that central island. However, the path to it is not straightforward. You will need to navigate through a series of trials to reach the heart and restore its magic."

Lily took a deep breath and set out along the winding path through the floating gardens. The path led her through a series of enchanting islands, each presenting its own unique challenges and wonders.

The first island she visited was filled with a dense, magical fog that obscured her vision. As she ventured into the fog, she noticed that the air was filled with floating, glowing orbs. The orbs seemed to guide her, and she realized that they were the key to navigating through the fog. By following the orbs, she found her way to a clearing where a small, shimmering pool of water rested. The water was clear and still, reflecting the light of the floating orbs.

At the edge of the pool was a message inscribed on a stone tablet. The message read: "To clear the fog and find your way, offer a wish from your heart and let your intentions guide you."

Lily closed her eyes and made a heartfelt wish for the restoration of the Heart of the Garden and the return of harmony to the Floating Gardens. As she spoke her wish, the fog began to dissipate, revealing a path that led to the next island.

The next island was home to a large, ancient tree with a hollow trunk. Inside the hollow, she found a series of puzzles and riddles inscribed on the walls. The puzzles required her to use her knowledge and intuition to solve them, and each solution revealed a piece of a magical map.

With each puzzle she solved, the magical map became clearer, guiding her toward the central island where the Heart of the Garden was located. As she completed the final puzzle, the map led her to a portal, which shimmered with a bright, inviting light.

Stepping through the portal, Lily arrived at the central island, where the Heart of the Garden was located. The island was more magnificent than any she had seen before. It was covered in lush, vibrant flora, and the air was filled with a gentle, harmonious melody.

In the center of the island stood a grand, ancient garden with an ornate fountain. The fountain's waters were still, and the once-glowing garden seemed dim and lifeless. The Heart of the Garden was a large, radiant crystal embedded in the center of the garden. It was dull and faint, its magic almost completely depleted.

Lily approached the Heart of the Garden and placed her hands on the crystal. She closed her eyes and focused on the wish she had made earlier. She imagined the gardens restored to their full beauty and harmony, and she felt a surge of warmth and energy flow through her.

As she concentrated, the crystal began to glow with a soft, golden light. The light grew brighter and more intense, and the garden around her started to come alive. The flowers bloomed, the trees rustled with joy, and the fountain's waters began to flow once more.

The magic of the Heart of the Garden was being restored, and with it, the harmony of the Floating Gardens. The islands began to move back into their proper positions, and the once-drifting landscapes were now aligned in perfect balance.

Petal, the talking flower, appeared beside her, its petals glowing with gratitude. "You have done it, Lily! The Heart of the Garden is restored, and the Floating Gardens are in harmony once more. Thank you for your courage and your kindness."

Lily smiled, feeling a deep sense of fulfillment. "I am glad I could help. The Floating Gardens are truly magical, and it is wonderful to see them restored."

With the Heart of the Garden's magic restored and the Floating Gardens back in harmony, Lily prepared to continue her journey. The pink balloon awaited her, ready to carry her onward to the next adventure in the Cloud Kingdom.

As she ascended into the sky, she looked back at the Floating Gardens with a sense of accomplishment. The gardens were now vibrant and full of life, and she knew that her efforts had made a difference.

With the pink balloon floating gently beneath her, Lily set her sights on the horizon, eager to discover the next wonder and challenge that awaited her in the magical realm above the clouds.

Chapter 10: The Starlit Summit

The pink balloon drifted serenely through the sky, carrying Lily away from the Floating Gardens and toward new horizons. As she floated, the clouds below seemed to shimmer with the colors of twilight, gradually giving way to a darkening sky studded with twinkling stars. The journey had been incredible, and Lily felt a sense of excitement for what lay ahead.

Soon, the balloon approached a majestic mountain range with peaks that reached high into the night sky. The highest peak was bathed in the soft, silvery light of the moon, and Lily could see that it was covered in a layer of glittering, stardust-like snow. The mountain had an ethereal, almost magical quality, and it seemed to beckon her onward.

As the balloon descended toward the mountain, Lily felt a sense of wonder. The peak of the mountain appeared to be adorned with a glowing constellation, as if the stars themselves had descended to touch the earth. The light from the stars cast a gentle, shimmering glow on the snow-covered slopes.

The balloon touched down on a smooth, snow-covered ledge near the base of the mountain. Lily stepped out and took a deep breath of the crisp, cool air. The night sky was clear and filled with an endless expanse of stars. The scene was breathtakingly beautiful, and she felt a sense of peace and awe.

A soft, melodic voice spoke from the shadows. "Welcome to the Starlit Summit, brave traveler."

Lily turned to see a graceful figure emerging from the shadows. The figure was a wise, ancient being with a flowing cloak that seemed to be made of starlight. Its eyes sparkled with the light of the stars, and its presence radiated a calm and dignified aura.

"I am Astra, the Guardian of the Starlit Summit," the being said with a warm, welcoming smile. "I have been expecting you."

Lily bowed slightly in respect. "Thank you, Astra. This place is truly magical. What brings me to the Starlit Summit?"

Astra's eyes twinkled with a knowing light. "The Starlit Summit is the final realm in your journey through the Cloud Kingdom. It is here that you will discover the true meaning of your adventure and unlock the ultimate gift of the Cloud Kingdom. To do so, you must complete the final trial, which is to reach the Summit of Stars."

Lily felt a surge of excitement and determination. "What do I need to do to reach the Summit of Stars?"

Astra gestured toward a narrow, winding path that led up the mountain. "The path to the Summit of Stars is challenging. You will face tests of courage, perseverance, and wisdom as you ascend the mountain. Along the way, you will encounter various trials that will test your resolve and the strength of your heart."

Lily nodded, ready to face the final trial. "I'm ready to begin."

With Astra's guidance, Lily set out along the winding path up the mountain. The ascent was steep and challenging, but Lily's determination kept her going. The path was illuminated by the soft glow of stardust and the light of the stars above. The higher she climbed, the more breathtaking the views became.

As she climbed, Lily encountered her first trial: a vast chasm that stretched across the path. The chasm was too wide to jump across, and the air was filled with swirling, icy winds. On the other side of the chasm, she could see a shimmering bridge made of starlight, but it was too far away to reach.

Lily took a deep breath and focused on the bridge. She remembered the lessons she had learned throughout her journey—the importance of courage and belief in oneself. With determination, she began to use the stardust she had gathered from the Floating Gardens to create a path of glowing stepping stones across the chasm.

As she carefully placed each stone, the path began to form, and the bridge of starlight appeared to become closer. With each step, she felt a sense of empowerment and hope. Finally, she reached the other side, where the bridge led her to the next stage of her ascent.

The next trial awaited her: a series of towering, crystalline spires that blocked her path. The spires were sharp and treacherous, and the only way through was to navigate a series of narrow gaps between them. The light from the stars reflected off the crystals, creating dazzling but disorienting patterns.

Lily took her time, carefully planning her route through the spires. She used her knowledge and intuition to find the safest path, stepping with precision and grace. The spires were challenging, but Lily's focus and determination guided her through.

As she emerged from the spires, she reached a plateau where a magnificent celestial observatory stood. The observatory was adorned with intricate celestial maps and charts, and a large, glowing telescope pointed toward the night sky.

At the center of the observatory was a celestial map, with a large, empty space where a star-shaped gem was meant to be placed. Astra appeared beside her; his eyes filled with encouragement.

"To reach the Summit of Stars, you must find the Star of Destiny and place it in the celestial map," Astra explained. "The Star of Destiny is hidden among the constellations. Use the telescope to find it."

Lily approached the telescope and peered through the lens. The telescope revealed a vast, sparkling array of stars, each one contributing to a grand celestial tapestry. As she adjusted the telescope, she saw a hidden constellation—an intricate pattern that resembled the Star of Destiny.

With Astra's guidance, Lily followed the constellation's pattern and found the hidden gem, glowing softly among the stars. She carefully retrieved the gem and returned to the celestial map. As she placed the Star of Destiny in its rightful place, the map illuminated with a brilliant, golden light.

The light from the map spread throughout the observatory, and the mountain began to glow with a soft, magical radiance. The path to the Summit of Stars was revealed, and Lily saw the final ascent leading to the highest peak.

With a heart full of gratitude and a sense of fulfillment, Lily made her way to the Summit of Stars. As she reached the peak, she was greeted by a breathtaking sight—the entire Cloud Kingdom spread out before her, illuminated by the light of countless stars. The view was awe-inspiring, and the sense of accomplishment was overwhelming.

Astra appeared beside her; his eyes filled with pride. "You have completed your journey and reached the Summit of Stars. You have proven your courage, wisdom, and kindness. The Cloud Kingdom is now forever changed by your presence."

Lily looked out at the beautiful, magical realm below. She felt a deep sense of peace and connection with the Cloud Kingdom and its wonders. The journey had been incredible, and she knew that the magic of the Cloud Kingdom would remain with her always.

As she prepared to descend from the summit, she felt a renewed sense of purpose and hope. The adventures she had experienced and the lessons she had learned would guide her in all the journeys yet to come.

With a final glance at the Summit of Stars and a heart full of gratitude, Lily climbed back into the pink balloon. As it floated gently down toward the Cloud Kingdom, she looked forward to the next chapter of her life, knowing that the magic of her adventure would always be a part of her.

And so, with the stars shining brightly above and the promise of new adventures ahead, Lily continued her journey, ready to embrace the future with courage and hope.

Chapter 11: The Return of the Pink Balloon

As the pink balloon floated gracefully from the Summit of Stars, Lily felt a mix of excitement and nostalgia. Her journey through the Cloud Kingdom had been filled with incredible adventures, profound lessons, and magical experiences. Yet, she knew it was time to return to her world and share what she had learned.

The balloon glided smoothly through the sky, descending gently toward the familiar landscapes of the Cloud Kingdom. The stars above twinkled like a thousand tiny lanterns, casting a serene light over the land. Lily looked out at the breathtaking beauty below, taking in the lush forests, shimmering rivers, and the enchanting Cloud Kingdom she had come to love.

As she approached the landing spot near the edge of the Cloud Kingdom, the pink balloon touched down softly on a grassy meadow. The meadow was filled with vibrant flowers and lush greenery, a picturesque reminder of the Floating Gardens she had visited earlier.

Lily stepped out of the balloon, her heart filled with a sense of fulfillment and peace. She knew that her journey had come full circle, and it was time to say goodbye to the magical realm she had explored.

Suddenly, a gentle breeze rustled through the meadow, carrying with it the soft, melodious sound of familiar voices. Lily turned to see a group of her friends and the magical creatures she had encountered throughout her adventures approaching her. Petal, the talking flower, Astra, the Guardian of the Starlit Summit, and other inhabitants of the Cloud Kingdom gathered around her, their faces beaming with joy.

"Welcome back, Lily!" Petal called out, its petals glowing with happiness. "We're so glad to see you again."

Astra smiled warmly as he approached. "You have accomplished great things on your journey. The Cloud Kingdom will always remember your bravery and kindness."

Lily felt a lump in her throat, touched by their words. "Thank you all for your support and guidance. This journey has been incredible, and I have learned so much from each of you."

The magical creatures and friends gathered around her, celebrating the success of her adventure. They presented her with a beautiful, shimmering gift—a small, enchanted locket that glowed with a soft, golden light.

"This locket is a token of our gratitude," Astra explained. "It contains a piece of the magic from the Cloud Kingdom. Whenever you wear it, it will remind you of the wonders you have experienced and the friendships you have made."

Lily accepted the locket with tears of joy in her eyes. "Thank you. I will treasure it always."

As the sun began to set, casting a golden glow over the meadow, Lily and her friend's shared stories, laughter, and fond memories of their time together. The sky was painted with hues of orange and pink, creating a picturesque backdrop for their celebration.

The time came for Lily to prepare for her departure. She climbed back into the pink balloon, feeling a sense of bittersweet farewell. The magical creatures and friends gathered around, waving, and cheering as the balloon began to lift into the sky.

With one last look at the Cloud Kingdom, Lily felt a deep sense of gratitude and wonder. The adventures she had experienced, the challenges she had overcome, and the magic she had witnessed would always hold a special place in her heart.

As the pink balloon ascended into the sky, Lily looked out at the horizon, ready to return to her own world with a heart full of memories and a spirit touched by magic. The journey had been extraordinary, and she knew that the lessons and experiences would guide her in all the adventures yet to come.

The balloon floated gently through the sky, carrying Lily toward her next chapter. The stars above twinkled like friendly eyes, watching over her as she embarked on a new journey. The magic of the Cloud Kingdom was now a part of her, and she was ready to embrace whatever the future held with courage and hope.

And so, as the pink balloon drifted toward the distant horizon, Lily's heart was filled with a sense of wonder and anticipation for the adventures that awaited her. The Cloud Kingdom had left an indelible mark on her soul, and she was ready to carry its magic with her wherever she went.

Chapter 12: The Echoing Horizons

As the pink balloon soared gracefully over the horizon, Lily's heart was a whirlwind of emotions. The magic of the Cloud Kingdom had woven its way into her very soul, and the thought of returning to her world with such wondrous experiences was exhilarating. The stars above seemed to twinkle with anticipation, and the balloon felt lighter, almost as if it were eager to continue its journey.

The sky began to change as the colors of twilight deepened into the rich, velvety hues of night. The balloon floated toward a new, exciting landscape that Lily had not seen before—an expansive realm of rolling hills, shimmering lakes, and vibrant, ever-changing skies. The air was filled with a sense of electric possibility.

Suddenly, the balloon's basket began to vibrate gently. Lily looked down and saw the fabric of the balloon shimmering with a radiant, golden light. The light seemed to pulse with rhythm, as if the balloon itself were responding to the magic around it. Her excitement grew—something extraordinary was happening.

The balloon began to glide effortlessly through the sky, moving faster and with a newfound energy. The landscape below seemed to blur and shift, revealing a series of spectacular sights. Floating islands with cascading waterfalls, fields of glowing flowers, and rivers of liquid light created a dazzling panorama of wonder.

As Lily gazed in awe, the balloon approached a grand, mystical structure rising majestically from the horizon. It was a colossal, sparkling archway made of crystalline material, glowing with an otherworldly light. The archway was adorned with intricate patterns that seemed to shift and dance in the light.

With a sense of wonder, Lily guided the balloon toward the archway. As the balloon passed through the arch, the light enveloped her in a warm, embracing glow. She felt a surge of energy and excitement, as if the very air around her were alive with magic.

Beyond the archway lay a breathtaking realm—a vibrant, echoing world where the landscape shifted and transformed with every step. The sky was a canvas of shifting colors, and the ground beneath her feet seemed to ripple with the rhythm of the universe. The atmosphere was charged with a sense of possibility and adventure.

The balloon landed gently on a floating platform that hovered above an endless, sparkling sea of stardust. The platform was adorned with luminous crystals and magical symbols, and a winding staircase led upward to a grand, celestial palace.

Lily stepped out of the balloon and ascended the staircase, her excitement growing with each step. The palace was a magnificent structure of gleaming, crystalline towers, and ethereal, shimmering walls. The interior was filled with floating lights and magical artifacts, and the air was filled with a harmonious melody that resonated throughout the palace.

At the heart of the palace was a grand, opulent chamber with a towering, celestial throne. Seated on the throne was a regal figure—an ancient and majestic being with an aura of radiant power. The figure's eyes sparkled with the light of a thousand stars, and its presence commanded both respect and awe.

"Welcome, Lily, to the Echoing Horizons," the being said in a voice that reverberated with cosmic energy. "I am Celestia, the Guardian of this realm. You have journeyed far and accomplished great deeds. The Echoing Horizons are a place of celebration and discovery, where the echoes of your adventures will resonate and reveal new wonders."

Lily felt a thrill of excitement. "It is an honor to be here, Celestia. What awaits me in the Echoing Horizons?"

Celestia's eyes glowed with a warm, inviting light. "In this realm, you will experience the culmination of your journey. The echoes of your adventures will manifest in ways you have never imagined. You will find answers to questions you did not know you had and discover new paths of adventure."

As Celestia spoke, the chamber began to transform. The walls shimmered and shifted, revealing scenes from Lily's journey—glimpses of the Floating

Gardens, the Whispering Caves, the Summit of Stars, and all the magical experiences she had encountered. Each scene was vibrant and alive, resonating with the energy of her adventures.

The echoes of the past began to interact with the present. The floating lights in the palace transformed into shimmering constellations, each one telling a story of its own. The stardust sea below the palace shimmered with patterns and symbols, creating a cosmic tapestry of wonder.

Celestia gestured toward a large, glowing orb in the center of the chamber. "This is the Orb of Echoes. It holds the essence of your journey and the magic of the Echoing Horizons. Place your hand upon it, and you will unlock the full potential of your adventure."

With a sense of anticipation, Lily approached the Orb of Echoes and placed her hand upon its surface. The orb glowed with a brilliant light, and the energy of her journey flowed through her. She felt a surge of insight and inspiration, and a vision of new possibilities unfolded before her eyes.

The vision revealed a series of new adventures and challenges, each one more exciting and extraordinary than the last. The Echoing Horizons had shown her that the magic of her journey was not just a destination but a continuous, ever-evolving adventure.

Celestia smiled, sensing Lily's newfound excitement. "The Echoing Horizons have revealed the boundless possibilities of your journey. The magic you have experienced is now a part of you, and it will guide you in all your future adventures."

Lily's heart was filled with a sense of exhilaration and joy. The realm of the Echoing Horizons had opened her eyes to the endless potential of her journey, and she felt more ready than ever to embrace whatever lay ahead.

As the stardust sea below sparkled with renewed brilliance, Lily prepared to continue her adventure. The pink balloon awaited her, ready to carry her to new realms and discoveries. With a heart full of excitement and wonder, Lily stepped back into the balloon and set her sights on the horizon.

The balloon ascended into the sky, carrying Lily toward new adventures and the endless echoes of her magical journey. The stars above seemed to shine even brighter, and the promise of discovery and excitement filled the air.

With each passing moment, Lily knew that the adventure was far from over. The Echoing Horizons had shown her that the magic of the journey was a living, breathing force, and she was eager to explore its boundless potential.

And so, as the pink balloon floated into the night sky, Lily's spirit soared with anticipation for the countless adventures that awaited her. The journey continued, and the echoes of her adventures would guide her through every new discovery and wonder.

Chapter 13: The Festival of Stars

The pink balloon glided through the starlit sky, carrying Lily away from the Echoing Horizons and toward her next adventure. The air was filled with a sense of anticipation, and the stars seemed to twinkle with excitement, as if they were eager to share a new wonder with her.

As the balloon descended, Lily saw a breathtaking spectacle below—a grand, celestial festival unfolding across a sprawling, enchanted landscape. The festival, known as the Festival of Stars, was a celebration of magic, wonder, and the boundless possibilities of the universe.

The ground was illuminated by thousands of glowing lanterns, each one floating gently in the air or resting on the surface below. The lanterns came in every color imaginable, casting a vibrant, multi-hued light that danced and shimmered with the rhythm of the festival. Stalls and pavilions adorned with shimmering fabrics and twinkling lights lined the pathways, offering a variety of magical delights and wonders.

The sky above was alive with an array of spectacular fireworks—dazzling displays of light and color that painted the heavens with radiant patterns. The constellations themselves seemed to join in the celebration, forming dazzling shapes and patterns that added to the festival's grandeur.

As the balloon touched down in the heart of the festival, Lily was greeted by a burst of joyous music and laughter. The air was filled with the sounds of lively melodies played by celestial musicians, and the scent of sweet, fragrant treats wafted through the air. The atmosphere was vibrant and festive, and Lily felt a thrill of excitement as she stepped out of the balloon.

A group of friendly, magical beings approached her—elegant, starry-eyed fairies with shimmering wings and warm smiles. They greeted her with enthusiastic cheers and invited her to join the festivities.

"Welcome to the Festival of Stars!" one of the fairies said with a twinkle in her eye. "We have been waiting for you. Tonight, the stars shine brighter than ever, and we have many wonders in store for you."

Lily's eyes sparkled with curiosity and delight. "Thank you! This festival is amazing. What can I experience here?"

The fairy giggled and fluttered her wings. "Oh, there is so much to see and do! From magical performances and enchanting games to celestial treats and dazzling displays, the Festival of Stars has something for everyone. And do not miss the grand star parade—it is the highlight of the evening!"

Excited by the prospect of the festival, Lily joined the fairies as they led her through the festival grounds. She marveled at the variety of magical experiences that awaited her.

First, she visited a pavilion where celestial performers dazzled the crowd with their incredible talents. There were acrobats soaring through the air with trails of stardust, musicians playing enchanting melodies on otherworldly instruments, and illusionists creating mesmerizing illusions that left the audience in awe.

Next, Lily explored the stalls, each offering unique and delightful treats. She sampled sparkling starfruit, shimmering mooncakes, and cosmic cotton candy that changed colors with each bite. The flavors were as magical as they were delicious, and Lily could not help but savor each delightful treat.

As the evening progressed, the fairies led her to a grand, open area where a massive, illuminated stage had been set up. The stage was adorned with twinkling lights and celestial decorations, and the audience was gathered in eager anticipation.

The grand star parade was about to begin.

Lily found a perfect spot to watch, and as the parade commenced, she was treated to a breathtaking display of magic and wonder. The parade featured magnificent floats adorned with glowing constellations, floating lanterns, and enchanting creatures from across the cosmos. Each float told a story of its own, celebrating the beauty and magic of the universe.

The highlight of the parade was a float featuring a stunning celestial tapestry—an intricate weaving of stars, galaxies, and cosmic wonders. The tapestry seemed to come to life, with stars twinkling and constellations shifting as the float moved through the parade.

Lily's heart was filled with joy and wonder as she watched the parade unfold. The Festival of Stars was truly a celebration of the universe's magic and beauty, and she felt grateful to be a part of it.

As the parade came to an end, the fairies gathered around Lily and presented her with a special gift—a beautiful, star-shaped locket that glowed with a soft, golden light.

"This locket is a symbol of the Festival of Stars," one of the fairies explained. "It holds a piece of the festival's magic and will remind you of the wonders you've experienced here."

Lily accepted the locket with a heartfelt thank you. "It is beautiful. I will cherish it always."

The festival continued into the night, filled with laughter, music, and celebration. Lily enjoyed every moment, dancing under the stars and making new friends among the magical beings of the festival.

As the night ended, Lily felt a sense of contentment and joy. The Festival of Stars had been a magical and unforgettable experience, and she knew that the memories of the evening would stay with her forever.

With the festival winding down and the first light of dawn beginning to appear, Lily prepared to continue her journey. The pink balloon awaited her, ready to carry her to new adventures and discoveries.

As she took one last look at the enchanting festival, Lily felt a renewed sense of wonder and excitement. The magic of the Festival of Stars had filled her heart with joy, and she was eager to see what new adventures awaited her.

With the stars twinkling brightly above and the festival's light fading into the distance, Lily climbed back into the pink balloon, ready to embrace the next chapter of her journey.

The balloon ascended into the sky, carrying Lily toward new horizons and the endless possibilities of her magical adventure. The Festival of Stars had been a celebration of wonder, and she was ready to continue exploring the magic of the universe with a heart full of hope and excitement.

Chapter 14: The Enchanted Mirage

As the pink balloon drifted away from the Festival of Stars, Lily felt a heartwarming sense of joy and contentment. The night sky stretched out before her, filled with endless possibilities and the promise of new wonders. The magical realm she had just left was still fresh in her mind, and she wondered what extraordinary adventures awaited her next.

The balloon sailed through a tranquil, moonlit sky, its gentle swaying soothing and calming. The air was filled with the soft hum of magic, and the stars seemed to guide the balloon toward a new and exciting destination.

After a while, the balloon descended gently into a land bathed in a soft, golden glow. As Lily looked out, she saw a breathtaking sight—a vast, shimmering desert with dunes that sparkled like diamonds under the moonlight. The desert seemed to stretch on forever, with the occasional oasis of lush greenery and blooming flowers dotting the landscape.

The balloon landed softly on a sandy dune, and Lily stepped out, feeling the warm, velvety sand beneath her feet. The desert was alive with a sense of magic and wonder, and she felt a thrill of excitement as she began to explore.

As Lily wandered through the desert, she noticed a series of intricate, glowing patterns etched into the sand. The patterns seemed to pulse with a gentle rhythm, creating a mesmerizing display of light and color. Intrigued, Lily followed the patterns, which led her to a magnificent, ancient archway made of shimmering, golden sandstone.

The archway was adorned with magical symbols and glowing runes, and it seemed to hum with an enchanting energy. Lily approached the archway, her curiosity piqued. As she stepped through, she found herself in a lush, magical oasis—a hidden paradise within the desert.

The oasis was a vibrant, verdant paradise, with crystal-clear pools of water, lush greenery, and flowers that glowed with a soft, iridescent light. The air was filled with the sweet scent of blooming flowers and the soothing sound of cascading water. In the center of the oasis was a majestic, ancient tree with golden leaves that shimmered in the sunlight.

Beneath the tree was a large, ornate mirror framed with intricate, magical designs. The mirror's surface was a swirling, shimmering pool of light, and it seemed to beckon Lily closer. As she approached the mirror, she noticed a curious inscription on the frame:

"To those who seek the heart of magic, the Enchanted Mirage will reveal its true essence."

Lily's heart raced with anticipation. She touched the surface of the mirror, and it began to glow with a radiant, golden light. The mirror's surface rippled, and an image began to take shape—a vision of a beautiful, otherworldly realm, filled with floating islands, crystalline waterfalls, and vibrant, magical creatures.

The vision began to shift and change, revealing glimpses of a grand celebration—a joyous, magical festival unlike any she had ever seen. The festival was filled with laughter, music, and dazzling displays of magic, and the entire realm seemed to be alive with happiness and wonder.

As the vision continued, Lily saw a magnificent, radiant being at the center of the celebration—a majestic figure with a glowing aura and a warm, welcoming smile. The figure seemed to embody the essence of joy and magic, and Lily felt an overwhelming sense of happiness and connection.

Suddenly, the vision shifted to focus on Lily herself. The mirror revealed a scene of her dancing joyfully amidst the magical festivities, surrounded by new friends and delightful creatures. The image was filled with laughter, joy, and a sense of profound contentment.

The mirror's surface shimmered and sparkled, and the vision faded to reveal a beautiful, glowing invitation. The invitation was adorned with sparkling stars and intricate patterns, and it read:

"You are cordially invited to the Heart of Magic—a celebration of pure joy and wonder. Your presence is the final touch that will complete the Enchanted Mirage."

Lily felt a surge of excitement and happiness. She had been invited to the Heart of Magic, and the prospect of experiencing such a celebration filled her with delight. With a sense of anticipation, she followed the invitation's guidance and began to explore the oasis further.

The golden tree in the center of the oasis seemed to hold the key to the celebration. As Lily approached, the tree's branches swayed gently, and a soft, melodic tune began to play. The golden leaves rustled, creating a beautiful, harmonious melody that resonated throughout the oasis.

The tree's trunk opened to reveal a hidden, glowing passageway. Lily stepped into the passageway, which was illuminated by a warm, golden light. The passage led to a stunning, enchanted realm—a magical world of floating islands, shimmering waterfalls, and radiant creatures.

The realm was alive with a sense of pure joy and wonder. Lily saw fantastical creatures of all shapes and sizes, each one adding to the vibrant tapestry of the celebration. The air was filled with the sounds of laughter, music, and cheerful chatter.

At the heart of the realm was a grand, glowing palace—a magnificent structure adorned with sparkling crystals and radiant lights. The palace was surrounded by a shimmering, magical aura, and it seemed to be the epicenter of the celebration.

As Lily entered the palace, she was greeted by a host of magical beings—fairies, enchanted creatures, and celestial beings—all celebrating with boundless joy. They welcomed her with open arms, and the festivities continued with a grand feast, dazzling performances, and joyful dances.

The central figure of the celebration, the majestic being from the mirror's vision, approached Lily with a warm, radiant smile. "Welcome to the Heart of Magic, dear traveler. Your presence has completed the Enchanted Mirage, and we are delighted to celebrate this joyous occasion with you."

Lily's heart was filled with pure happiness as she joined in the celebration. The magic of the Heart of Magic had truly transformed the realm into a wondrous, joyful place, and she felt a deep sense of connection and fulfillment.

As the night wore on and the festivities continued, Lily felt a sense of gratitude and wonder. The Heart of Magic had revealed the true essence of joy and enchantment, and she knew that this magical experience would stay with her forever.

With a heart full of happiness and a spirit uplifted by the celebration, Lily prepared to continue her journey. The pink balloon awaited her, ready to carry her to new horizons and adventures.

As she looked back at the Heart of Magic, Lily felt a profound sense of contentment and joy. The magic of the Enchanted Mirage had been a beautiful, unforgettable experience, and she was eager to see where her next adventure would lead.

With a final, joyous farewell to the magical realm, Lily climbed back into the pink balloon, ready to embrace the next chapter of her journey with a heart full of happiness and wonder.

The balloon ascended into the sky, carrying Lily toward new adventures and the endless possibilities of her magical journey. The Heart of Magic had been a celebration of pure joy, and she was excited to continue exploring the wonders of the universe with a heart full of hope and excitement.

Chapter 15: The Journey's End

As the pink balloon soared gracefully through the sky, Lily gazed out at the vast expanse of the universe stretching before her. The magic of her journey had been nothing short of extraordinary, and she felt a deep sense of fulfillment and wonder. Her heart was full of cherished memories, and the stars seemed to shine with a special light, guiding her toward the last destination of her incredible adventure.

The balloon floated gently toward a serene, tranquil realm—a land where the sky was a canvas of soft pastels, and the air was filled with a sense of peace and harmony. The landscape below was a breathtaking mosaic of rolling hills, blooming meadows, and crystal-clear lakes. It was a place that seemed to embody the essence of tranquility and magic.

As the balloon descended and touched down on a lush, verdant hill, Lily stepped out and took a deep breath of the fresh, fragrant air. The gentle breeze rustled through the tall, graceful grasses, and the sky above was a serene, pastel canvas, dotted with wispy clouds.

In the distance, Lily saw a magnificent, golden gate standing at the entrance of a beautiful, majestic garden. The gate was adorned with intricate patterns and shimmering, magical symbols, and it seemed to beckon her with a warm, inviting glow.

With a sense of wonder and anticipation, Lily approached the golden gate. As she stepped through, she found herself in a breathtaking, enchanted garden—a realm of unparalleled beauty and serenity. The garden was filled with vibrant, blooming flowers, crystal-clear streams, and towering, ancient trees with golden leaves.

At the heart of the garden was a grand, radiant pavilion, where a host of familiar faces awaited her. The magical beings, creatures, and friends she had encountered throughout her journey had gathered to celebrate the culmination of her adventure. Petal, Astra, the fairies, and many others stood with warm smiles and open arms.

"Welcome, Lily," Petal said with a joyful twinkle in its petals. "You've come to the final destination of your journey, and we're honored to share this moment with you."

Astra nodded with a proud smile. "Your journey has been remarkable, and you have shown great bravery, kindness, and wonder. This is a celebration of all you have accomplished."

Lily felt a surge of emotion as she looked around at her friends and companions. "Thank you all. This journey has been incredible, and I am grateful for every moment."

The celebration in the enchanted garden was filled with joy and laughter. The pavilion was adorned with magical decorations and shimmering lights, creating a warm and inviting atmosphere. The garden was alive with music, dance, and a feast of delightful treats and celestial delicacies.

As the festivities continued, Lily took a moment to reflect on her journey. She thought about the Cloud Kingdom, the Festival of Stars, the Enchanted Mirage, and all the magical experiences she had encountered. Each adventure had taught her valuable lessons and filled her heart with wonder.

At the center of the pavilion, a grand, shimmering book was presented to Lily. The book was adorned with golden lettering and intricate designs, and its pages glowed with a soft, magical light.

"This is the Book of Adventures," Astra explained. "It holds the stories of your journey and the magic you have experienced. It is a testament to the wonders you have encountered and the joy you have brought to the world."

Lily opened the book, and its pages began to turn, revealing beautifully illustrated depictions of her adventures. Each page was a vibrant and enchanting representation of the places she had visited, the friends she had made, and the magic she had witnessed.

As she turned the final page, she saw a heartfelt message written in shimmering, golden script:

"Dear Lily, your journey has been a celebration of magic, wonder, and joy. You have touched the hearts of many and embraced the true essence of adventure. May your spirit continue to shine brightly, and may you always find joy and wonder in every step of your journey."

Lily's heart swelled with gratitude and happiness. The Book of Adventures was a beautiful reminder of the magic she had experienced, and she knew it would be a cherished keepsake for years to come.

As the celebration continued, Lily felt a deep sense of contentment and fulfillment. Her journey had ended, but the magic and memories would remain with her forever.

With a final, joyful farewell to her friends and companions, Lily prepared to return to her own world. The pink balloon awaited her, ready to carry her back home. As she climbed into the balloon, she took one last look at the enchanted garden, feeling a profound sense of peace and gratitude.

The balloon ascended into the sky, carrying Lily toward the horizon and her own world. The stars above twinkled with a warm, reassuring light, and the sky was filled with a sense of endless possibilities.

As the balloon floated gently through the sky, Lily knew that the journey had been a remarkable adventure—one that had touched her heart and filled her life with magic. She was eager to return to her world with a spirit uplifted by wonder and a heart full of cherished memories.

And so, with a sense of fulfillment and joy, Lily's adventure came to an end. The magic of her journey had left an indelible mark on her soul, and she was ready to embrace whatever the future held with a heart full of hope and excitement.

The pink balloon continued its journey through the night sky, carrying Lily toward new beginnings and the endless possibilities of her magical life. The stars shone brightly, guiding her toward a future filled with wonder, joy, and the promise of new adventures.

The magical end.

Don't miss out!

Visit the website below and you can sign up to receive emails whenever Kirsten Yates publishes a new book. There's no charge and no obligation.

https://books2read.com/r/B-A-WIEEC-BGRLE

BOOKS2READ

Connecting independent readers to independent writers.